Stages of Love

C. R. Dunn

Stages of Love

Published by:

Anuzan Publications

ISBN:

For those who have inspired these emotions in me.

For good or ill, you have made me who I am.

Love

Cute Dates

Cute as a button,
So I be a stuttering,
I just wanted to say,
That it would make my day,
That you would say yes,
To playing some guess...who?

Family

I hate you,
I love you,
I don't even know.

I want you around,
But we always find a way,
To bring out the anger.

I don't even know,
Why we can't just be nice,
When we care deep down inside.

I guess this just is,
What it means to be,
A family.

Passion

A burning need,
The urge for release,
Why must I feel this all-consuming desire.

So overwhelmed inside my own mind,
Nothing that will help it stop,
Anything to make the noise go away.

The wrong choices are all I make,
Are you going to be another?

Building Courage

That little look,
Avoiding notice,
why can't I talk?

I want to know you,
But something holds me back,
Why must I be my own worst enemy.

I will try,
Maybe another day,
I don't know why I don't.....

New Years Eve

I wanted to talk,
I never could manage,
It was quarter to twelve,
And all my friends pushed.

I still couldn't do it,
I've known you for years,
But never could manage,
To admit how I feel.

It was getting closer to twelve,
Minute by minute,
So close to the drop,
I needed to try.

I steeled my resolve,
I would tell you then,
But I couldn't see,
Where you left to.

A tap at the shoulder,
Who would I find,
I could hear them all start,
To count down from 10.

Who did I find,
It was actually you,
I opened my mouth,
You stopped me at 2.

I brought in the year,
With my one true dream,
A beautiful girl,
Kissing me first.

Parts of Living

The things that make a life.

We have all,
Lived, Laughed and Loved.
Lost, Cried and Screamed.
Read, Wrote and Spoke.

We are able to do these things,
Because of those around us.
We may not communicate this,
The same way as others.
It's not always about what they see,
Or what they think they know.

It's what you feel inside,
Our ups and downs,
Our highs and lows.

Our feelings make living a life.

Painful Decisions

My breathing increases,
My heart rate rises,
Why am I so nervous?
Am I afraid to see you,
Or do I hope I do?
I won't know what to say,
I won't know what to do.
What are my options now?
Stay sober and hope like hell,
Or get drunk and do the same…

Wishful Thinking

That smile I want to be true,
I see it every time you look at me.
Or is it when I look at you?
We were so close,
But they threw us apart.
I want us to come back,
But I'm afraid of it going wrong.
Should I risk my sanity,
For one more chance?

Nights We Barely Remember

That wild night,
That thumping music.
It speeds the heart,
It quickens the mind.
I want to share it with you,
I want it to be true.
I danced with you,
I made it true.
We were as one,
We were a perfect moment.

Arguments

You push me,
You knead me,
You refuse to let up.

It's always my fault,
Never your own,
I'm always the monster.

Why can't you see,
That you're part of the problem,
What you say and I hear are two different
things.

You must never forget that,
There is more to the story,
There is a whole world,
between our minds

Why do I Even Try?

How can I tell you,
What I can't even tell myself.
Love is a dream,
That some have to chase.
I tried to stop running,
All my choices were wrong.
It is time to step back,
And learn to love myself.

Breathtaking View

The moon sits above,
Covering you in its glow.
The smile on your face,
Is my new favourite sight.
I don't want to move,
And break this moment too soon.
But I just can't resist,
Taking you in my arms.

Mad

I don't know what to say,

To make you feel better.

I don't know what I did,

To make you so mad.

I don't know what I'll do,

Without you in my life.

Broken

You say that you're broken,
But I don't care or listen.
You don't understand,
That we are all the same.
We are all affected,
By the doubt in our lives.
I may show a strong face,
But I'm just better at hiding it.

Left Me Behind

I want to be with you but you left me behind.
You've gone so far I can no longer see you,
You shine with the light of all those who love
you,
Your light so bright it covers me in shadow,
How can I come back when you have
surpassed me so?

Smile

It warmed my heart to see her smile,
The first time in forever that it looked real.

She bounced behind the bar,
With a life to her step,
Completely in control of her space.

It wasn't her looks that drew the eye,
It was the energy she put off,
Someone so entirely in the moment.

I wasn't sure if it was the alcohol,
That put the warmth in my cheeks.
I didn't think I cared.

Morpheus

My eyes droop as I force them open,
I refuse the call of Morpheus.
I wait to hear the sound of keys,
To know you're home and safe.
The thought of you out alone,
Fills me utterly with fear.
But now it's three,
And I hear you there.
It's time to go to sleep.

Lost Without You

I'd be lost without you.
Someone to push me up,
When I was at my lowest.
Someone to hold me up,
When I was at my highest.
Someone to keep me level,
When I would think too much.
Someone for me to help,
Through those same moments.
We never gave up,
Through thick and thin.
My friends.

Together

We started as two,
Together we were one,
Through our days of love and fun.

But we drifted apart,
while living our lives,
Only god knows how hard we tried.

We wish the other strength,
On the path through hell,
As we work out how to be well.

Smile

That cute little smile,
You show when you laugh.
The twinkle in your eye,
When you make fun of me.
You lean against me,
Like it wasn't a choice.
Makes me want to hold you,
For as long as I can.
Stay in my life,
Because it wouldn't be the same,
Without you there.

Opening Up

Just because I love you,
Doesn't mean I will open up,
Showing you who I really am,
Is just asking to be hurt.

Charming

I fell into your eyes,
Blue as the water,
Surrounding us both.

I knew it wouldn't work,
But I couldn't not try,
I swam through the ocean,
To get closer to you.

I strutted my way,
Out of the water,
Trying to feel like 007.
I leant on the bar,
And tried my best line.

You couldn't help laugh,
At this idiot you spent,
The rest of your life with.

Window to the Soul

Her eyes sparkled with an eerie light,
Colours that I had never seen before,
A depth that I could fall into without knowing.

My heart fluttered as I paused,
An unknown fear of approaching her,
Thundering through the reaches of my brain,
My heart is the braver one ignoring its call.

I surrendered myself,
Heart, mind and soul,
Unto this Goddess,
Bursting into my life.

Adorable

You are so cute,
Closing your eyes,
As I kiss your head,
The blush to your cheeks,
When I take your hand,
A catch in your breath,
As I pull you close.
All of these actions,
Are only part of the picture.

Emotion

Love is the most painful emotion,
It leaves us too open.

Facing the Past

How do I talk,
To someone I loved so much,
Only to be forgotten,
When she found someone different.
Once she was hurt,
I only became,
A symptom,
To what she endured.

Nervousness

The flutter in my chest,
When I don't know what to say,
As I see you walk,
Through those doors.

Unspoken Affection

Your warmth at my side,
Makes every moment special,
Whether we're watching a sunset,
Or reading a book on the couch.
You truly are my better half,
Lifting me up at my lows,
And relying on me when you fall,
You make my life greater,
Than the sum of its parts.

Balance

I don't know how,
My life would work,
Without your light,
To offset my darkness.
Without your innocence,
To temper my judgement,
I have become a better person,
With your support at my back.
I look forward to the future,
of us.

A Simple Action

When words fail,
The power of simple things are felt,
A single hug can change everything…

A Distance From Love

I miss you being you,
You've been through so much,
And you feel out of sorts.
I don't know how to help,
While you push me away,
I can only try to comfort,
you from here.

Caught Between

I don't know how to act,
When the two of you are,
At each other's throats.
How did I become the one in between,
Trying to placate you both,
I guess I have to act like the older brother.

A Missing Piece

When I'm alone,
I yearn for your touch.
My body feels colder,
When we can't be together.
We spent so long,
Being joined at the hip,
That I don't know what to do,
That that you've left.

Affection

It's the awkward little moments,
The affection is shown,
When the little bad jokes,
Almost become flirting,
But that line can't be crossed,
Because of a chasm of history,
Lies between those two points.

Social Media

I learnt something new today,
You're posting more,
While stuck at home.

How did I never see,
That beautiful flecks of grey,
In your piercing blue eyes.

We spend our days distracted,
By everything around us,
Forgetting the beauty close to us.

A Choice of Words

You see me for me,
And,
Only you can perceive,
The hidden depths,
Of my soul.
Can be seen the same,
If you feel the message of my story.

Don't Know What to Say

I know that I'm awkward,
Just wanting to talk,
I never seem to know,
What I should say,
I stare at your message,
Wanting to answer,
Stare at your name,
Wanting to call,
I just want to hear your voice.

Learning to Love You

I have a feeling,
It won't go away,
She's who I think of,
All of my day.

I think I'm in love,
I want to know,
I've always run before,
But I've tried to grow.

It's worth a shot,
Following this feeling,
I want to be shown,
How to love her.

Waking Up

You are the reason,
I love waking up in the morning.

Small Actions

A simple smile,
At the right time,
Can save a life.

Behind a Screen

Why do we judge so quick,
When did looks become personality,
It's hard to see who a person is,
When we see so little,
So many lies on a screen,
As necks are permanently on a lean,
I want to get to know you,
Away from the mobile.

Platonic Love

Can we hold hands as friends?
I just want to be close,
To who I care about,
Why does it have to be weird,
To show that affection,
In our actions as well as words.

The Storm

A raging storm,
Reminds me of you,
The flash of lightning,
Stunning in view,
The roar of thunder,
Pushing my chest,
The cascade of rain,
Caressing my skin,
Something so fleeting,
Leaving its mark.

Are You Still There?

I hope to see a small smile,
To show that you were still there,
To prove to yourself,
The strength you always had,
Hidden in your core,
That couldn't be diminished,
No matter how low you felt,
Or how they treated you.

Together

Love is what keeps us together,
Whether it be love of self,
Or love of another,
Love is what keeps us together.
Even if we fall,
We love to hate ourselves,
But still we try,
Love is what keeps us together.

Pain

Regret

Why does my chest hurt,
When I see you with him?

That sweet smile on your face,
That I couldn't create.

You walked away because I couldn't be,
The man that you held in your heart.

Why Did You Leave?

How could you leave
From something so dumb
Too much to drink
And now you are gone.

I keep looking up
Seeing your shadow
Just outside,
Waiting for me.

I wish I could hate you
For being so dumb
But I only can miss
That stupid smile.

I will never forgive
The loss of the life
That we should have had.

I can never forget
That heartbreaking pain
That came with that knock
That should have been you.

A Look of Regret

Why do you give me that look?
That one that says what you can't,
The one that I wish I couldn't understand.

Anxiety

Anxiety is why I wear a ring,
That little distraction when I need a hand.
Anxiety is why I wear a bracelet,
Something to move instead of running.
Anxiety is why I'm quiet,
When I'm not pretending to a customer.
Anxiety is why I always explain too much,
Always afraid you will turn your back.
Trust is how I move forward,
Past the anxiety that held me back.

I Still Feel You

The creak beneath the floors,
The rustle at the window,
It that you?

The breath through my hair,
The murmur behind the tv,
Is that you,
Trying to tell me something more?

I see when I'm dreaming,
I hear you as I lay awake,
Deep into the night,
I feel that you are near.

I want you to let me go,
I want to tend my life,
I wish for you to truly pass,
And stop following mine.

I loved your smile,
I missed your warmth,
I wish your memory would stop haunting me,
So I can live my life.

Gone But Still Present

You say you're there,
But how do I know?

Your eyes glaze,
You look past us all,
It's like we're nothing to you.

The moment is key,
You live in it with us,
Or the distance alone,
We can only reach so far.

A Wreck

I hate you for leaving me.

It should have been me,
Dead in that ditch,
Making bad choices
Driving that car.

But you had to be
The ever big hero,
Too wary for me
To see where you're going.

I will never forget
That moment they told me
Laying in bed
Too broken to move
That you had left me.

No reason to stay
Knowing I caused it
I think I just might
Finish what started.

Broken Little Heart

You think you know me?

Just wallowing in my shadow,
You only know what I show you.

Be it of my own will or not,
The face that I wear in the open.
Is but a construct,
Shielding me from the world.

I wish you could know
What truly dwells in my heart.

That heart that yearns for your warmth,
That warmth that could fix what I broke,
My broken little heart.

It broke for trying to love another,
Another that could not find,
A way to share that which was offered.

My broken little heart.

Anger Or Hate

Anger or Hate
I never could tell.

You're in my head
That learnt behaviour.

Making me "better"
Making me worse.

Making me "love"
Making me hate.

Follow your lead
Hating myself.

Wanting your love
Getting your scorn.

Wanting your truth
Getting your lies.

Why do I want
What you refuse.

Why do I need
That hate-filled love.

Why do I think
That you want love.

Why don't I know
The lies in your words.

Why can't I see
The pain in the end.

Only time will tell
How far I fall.

Forever Painful

The pain that won't go away,
Always spikes when I see you,
My agony won't abate,
Since my heart can't leave you.

The Question

I see the echo in your eye,
The pain you hide behind the smile,
The tear you wipe from your cheek.

The question you don't want to ask,
The choice that you shouldn't have.
Should I end this life I hate,
Or continue living?

I ask this of you my friend,
Please don't leave us,
Just because we don't have time,
Doesn't mean we want you gone.

With life,
Things can change.
If you leave,
Nothing will be as bright.

Walked Away

Footsteps in the sand,
As you walk away from me.

I stay as the surf washes them away,
Still on my knees where you left me.

My heart breaking into smaller pieces,
As the light leaves my life.

Dawn breaks as I trudge back,
To the home I wanted to be ours.

Alone

Always alone,
In places I don't know.
Surrounded by people,
That I don't understand.
Why has life turned out this way,
A journey that I didn't start.
I try to find those,
That I want near me.
It never turns out,
The way that I want.
They always seem,
To get further away.

Sleepless

Is it the creak in the wall,
Or the sound at my window,
That I'm blaming for,
Not sleeping tonight?

The thoughts in my head,
That go round and round,
Never letting me sleep,
Is probably the truth.

But I won't say that,
That would require admitting,
To what's actually there.

Gone

You can't be gone, I won't let you!
I refuse to think what life would be,
Without your soul entwined with mine,
Without your breath upon my neck,
Without your hands through my hair,
Without your warmth at my side,
You can't be gone, I won't lose you.

A Lost Dream

Your eyes shine,
Our gaze locks,
That awkward glance.

An unknown smile,
A tinge of fear,
My apprehension.

I come closer,
Do I speak?
You don't let me.

You are a dream,
Of one I lost,
Beyond the veil,
Already gone.

Painful Questions

I know you wonder,
Why I won't ask,
That question you've waited to hear.

It's because you walked away,
When I needed you most,
To go to him.

You know what he did,
He was never faithful,
To any of us.

He wasn't my friend,
He wasn't your partner,
He was just a traitor.

He knew that I loved you,
And used it against us,
And ruined us all.

YOU!

I wrote it about you,
But how could I tell you,
I never wanted to hurt you,
Yet was always hurt by you,
My thoughts were about you,
I'm at my worst with you,
I hated myself around you.

Do you see the problem?
It was always about you,
Never about me.

Why did I never think of me,
When you never deserved me,
I needed to grow me,
You needed to know about me,
The self hid by me,
I never should have lost me,
I need time to remember me.

Lost Love

As I look into the distance.
The waves crash at the,
Base of the cliffs below me.
I can hear a bird I don't recognise,
Singing in a new day.

But I can't seem to feel joy,
As a beautiful new day starts.
My pain makes the world grey,
As I remember the last time we,
Were here together.

Trust

The hardest part of being hurt,
Is not knowing how to trust,
Past experience pollute our minds,
Controlling how we act,
Creating a film across our eyes,
Which taints all that we see,
Part of growing as a person,
Is learning to put down our past,
And learning how to trust.

The Risk

Do we take that step forward?
Or stay as we are?
This isn't the first step,
But it could be our last.
I'm afraid of commitment,
You're wary of cheaters,
We are both broken,
But neither can tell,
Whether we'll build ourselves up,
Or destroy each other again.

This is not What I Wanted

I'm not who I wanted to be,
But the person you made me,
The comments and snide remarks,
Had me jumping through hoops,
That only existed in my mind.

I chose to close myself away,
From anyone who could help fix,
Those parts of me that you broke,
Without even seeming to try.

I have no choice but to give,
Living a real-life once again,
Being alone anymore,
Just might kill the part of me,
Reaching out for human contact.

Closer or Further Away?

I always wanted you closer,
But he made the first move,
I sit here watching you both in love.
As glad as I am to see people I love happy,
It still hurts when I remember,
That it could have been me,
I missed my only chance,
I know I have to move on,
But it gets harder,
Every time I see,
Both of you,
Together.

The Lies

I try to move past,
All the things that you did,
Be the "bigger man" they say,
But why should I have to?
Why am I the one,
Who has to fix what was broken,
To repair the jigsaw you ruined,
The former core of my being.
You got off scot-free,
Telling your "truth",
Painting me as the problem,
I'm trying to leave you behind,
But in those midnight hours,
It gets increasingly harder,
To not dwell back on that,
History we shared.

Pointless

I am a pointless machine,
A useless cog in the system,
A screw that holds together nothing,
A single piece that matters not,
A "person" that has no dialogue.
Every day stays the same,
Every time I try but nothing is better,
Every person is another that doesn't listen,
Every evening I go back to bed alone.
I want to break away,
I want to have a voice,
I want to influence you all,
I want you to walk away better.
One more day to grow,
One more time to let you know,
One more person I will try to not let down,
One last attempt to be better.
Unless you stop me, it will happen,
Unless I stop trying I will succeed,
Unless they listen they won't learn from my
mistakes,
Unless we work together we won't finish.
I won't be pointless anymore.

Fear

Fear is how we learn ourselves,
Do you cower, or do you fight?

The Nights We Regret

I made a mistake,
Ran into a girl,
That I was so in love with,
Sadness took over,
And I fell into the bottle,
I went to drive off,
But didn't make it far,
The flashing lights,
That proved my stupidity.

Resilience

How we made it to here,
With the pain we went through,
Those parts of our soul,
We break in lonely moments,
The fire in our hearts,
Barely dampened by the sorrow,
The wings on our back,
Not quite melting from the sun,
The steel in our spines,
Barely bent from the weight.
These small things,
That we barely acknowledge,
Are the strength of our body,
Overcoming our wounds.

Dodged

The time for me to disappear,
Was the first time I dodged.

Addiction

I fear for my soul,
When I feed an addiction.

The Path

My pain shows me,
Those events that I lived through.
My heart drags me,
Into places that I might regret.
My joy proves to me,
That my heart wasn't always wrong.
My soul pains me,
To prove that I'm still alive.

The Darker Side

Those moments when my mind wanders,
Even I'm not sure where it'll go,
Will it be my problems felt,
Or will it be my yearnings,
Too often it's the darker side,
And rarely to my hopes.

Communication

The words I say,
Aren't the words you hear,
This confusion hurts,
It may destroy our connection…

Afraid

I always feel like,
I'm going to hurt you.
Never intentionally,
But,
Somehow,
I'll do something,
Or say something,
That ruins everything.

Cold

As my eyes close without you there,
I feel a chill of cold,
It isn't the same being alone.

Monsters

The monster we hide inside,
Is the monster we fear unleashing.
The monsters we see around us,
Are the ones that can be ignored.

A False Face

A mask is what I wear,
When I enter the world,
I don't even know how,
To show my real self,
Always had to suppress,
What I felt or I thought,
The world is not kind,
To those who stand out.

Silence of an Empty Bed

This pain in my chest,
Since you went away,
It won't follow your lead,
And leave me to heal.
It grows more intense,
When I lay in my bed,
It's those moments of silence,
That I feel completely alone.

Silence

Silence
A contemplative moment,
Or one burdened by doubt,
So many facets to such a simple word,
Why am I afraid of this silence,
A silence while I wait for you,
What will your answer be?

Feel Safe

I don't want this to happen,
I don't want leave this place,
This place just started to feel safe,
Why did you change it,
By appearing again,
I'm always afraid,
Never alone in my head,
It's completely your fault,
I'm scared of myself,
I'm scared of damn near everything,
I just want to feel safe again…

Choices

I'm in a bad place now,
My heart slams in my chest.
I know how I got here,
I dug this hole myself.

It was my own bad choices,
That led me to this day.
I have to make it better,
Move on with my life.

I know you think I blame you,
But you just tried too hard.
I hope that you can see,
That we weren't right together.

We both need to grow,
And be our own people.

Touch Starved

My mood is so low,
I know what it's from,
My skin is so starved,
It just needs a touch,
From a close one's skin.
I've suffered before,
This isolating feeling,
Had pulled away,
From everyone around,
Needed that touch,
To stop this skin-starved feeling.

Broken or Not?

There are two questions,
The curious want to ask,
But know you're not allowed.
What broke you?
and
Did you recover?
They're both ones,
That are hard to be asked,
And even harder to answer.

Lost in Place

This isn't where I was supposed to be,
Somewhere I went off track,
Took the road less travelled,
And it led me here,
To a dead end.
I wanted to be more,
I wanted to learn,
But the drive was gone,
I don't know what to do.

My Old Self

I don't miss you,
I miss who I used to be,
The person I was,
Was so trusting,
I believed in people,
I KNEW who you were,
I,
Was,
Wrong…

Missing Love

Her heartaches,
Seeing his smile,
Remembering the times,
It was directed at her.

His cheeks hurt,
Forcing a smile,
Trying to pretend,
That he didn't see her.

Two people,
Pining for their past,
That they both,
Wish was the present.

What we see,
Is never the truth,
Only what others,
Project to the world.

Heavy Heart

Why does my heart feel heavy,
Without you in my life.

My Darkness

When the darker side comes,
Suddenly I'm broken,
Never a concern,
When the smile was token.
Can't open up,
Don't want to scare them,
Tryna be myself,
Time will show the outcome.

Cyberbullying

The wonder of technology,
Such joy can be shown,
Yet you use it to hurt,
You shame and bully,
And miss the beauty,
Contacting friends across the world,
Reaching out to those in need,
A simple selfie of a smile,
These mesmerising moments,
Forever saved in time,
And you want to use it to hurt…

Hidden Emotion

Here's a game to play,
Is my smile genuine,
Or am I hiding my fears?

Growth

Good Enough for Yourself

Other people don't get to decide whether you're enough,
You do.

You choose how far to go,
How much to be,
How little others see.

You speak for yourself,
You can hear what they say,
You decide how much to take.

Be yourself,
Look inside and decide,
That you are strong enough.

Why?

Why?
The question I always have to ask.

Why was I not enough?
Why wasn't I the one?
Why did you choose to do this?

But it's never the question I want,
The one I want is not even a question,
but statements.

I am good enough.
I am the one you walked away from.
I am the one you wronged.

Yes,
I am is what I want.

Walking Away

I watch you walk away,
Never sure why I didn't stop you.
My heartbreak,
Never knowing if I was wrong.

I spend years,
Never knowing if I should let you in.
On a whim,
Never pushing you away again.

Looking back,
Never doubting I made the right choice.

Progress

I am who I am,
Different from yesterday,
Maybe greater tomorrow,
Ever evolving.

Better Than Yesterday

I don't know who I want to be.
I only know I want to be better,
Than I was yesterday.

Just because I sometimes fall,
Doesn't mean I'm not trying,
Getting up is harder each time.

The dark feelings infect me,
The happy feelings raise me,
Equilibrium is never in sight.

I fell

Noone to catch me,
Noone to care,
Noone to watch.

As I lay,
I refuse to stop,
I refuse to stay,
I refuse to let
You think you control.

It wasn't my fault
No matter you say
I will be strong

I will move on
To be myself
Without you

The Storm

The scent of ozone in the air,
Mist upon my skin.
A rumble rolls across the sky,
A storm is coming in.

The winds are wild,
Rain is near,
My skin soaks it in.

I stand beneath the clouds up high,
And feel pure and clean once again.

Hope

That golden feeling,
Looking forward to life.

I can only believe,
That tomorrow will be better.

Bad things may happen,
But it keeps us all going.

When the sky is falling,
When nothing is right,
It's all we have left.
HOPE!

Be Better

I know what I want,
I want to be better,
My work to be greater,
My life to be fuller.

I know it's a process,
But I will not be stopped,
I will stand resolute,
And continue on my rise.

My Mind

Lost in a sea of my own mind,
Memories swirling around me,
Like a newly formed galaxy.

I wish I could push away,
The painful ones,
And pull close the pleasant.

Some days it truly feels like,
It would be safer to just be numb.

Good Man

How do I know if I'm a good person?
My whole life,
An endless loop of follow the leader,
Marching along to the tune of another's drum,
Never to know what truly makes me, me!
What opportunity can I have, when I'm
basically an NPC in a rich man's world.
How do I know if I'm a good man?
The feelings well up inside,
While I smile at the next person inline
My obligation to be a part of their world as
they are a part of mine
Never to know what's truly in their mind,
As they know nothing of mine
The questions of what, when, who and why
always running through our minds
Never to know where it's heading, high or low,
good or bad,
How do I KNOW if I'M a good Man?!

Coping

Coping with pain,
Why don't I complain?
I am afraid.
That you won't listen,
And let me drop back,
Into the bottle and pills.
I got out of that hole,
I don't want to go back.
That person is not,
Who I want to be.

Memories

Life is for the Living,
Death means nothing to the dead.
Grief is to miss those that left us,
Acceptance means you have started to move on.
I ask you to leave this stage of life to me,
I had no reason to miss you,
Yet somehow I did.
I've tried to move on with my life,
But the memories of you won't let me go.

The Depths of my Mind

The thoughts in my mind,
Are a mystery to even me.
Why can I never place,
Those feelings that I have.
They seem to come from nowhere,
And disappear into the ether,
From where they came.

Losing Touch

Where did you go,
My old friend?
It's been too long,
Since we have seen each other.
It wasn't our fault,
We tried so hard.
We drifted away,
To be "adults".
We did as they said,
We tried real hard,
But we're just kids,
Lost in a moment.

Not Where I Want to Be

Not feeling this place,
Don't even know why I'm here.
All the people suck,
It's always my fault.

All of these people,
Doing amazing things,
Making me want to do,
The wonderful things they are.

I'm stuck in a rut,
Paused in a moment.
Trying to be more,
Wanting to raise up.

Void

The void is where we start,
And the void is where we end,
Life is but a series of events in between,
Stories are how we judge those times,
Our highs are how we know we live,
Our lows are what give proof that we endure,
We can only hope to leave more highs,
In the eyes of those that saw our lows.

A Mistake

I didn't feel right this time,
As you committed this crime.
I should have seen it coming,
It should have been so obvious,
It was but a show of hands,
Something that I could not stand.
You all turned away from me,
I just waited for you to see,
Why I felt so alone,
Standing in this crowd unknown.
I finally realised I wasn't friends,
As you all left me to make amends.
I often look back on that day,
Upon which I walked away,
Knowing I would be ok,
Being a better man today.

Nothing to Me

I don't resent your actions anymore,
I'd have to still care for that,
I've done the very things you swore I couldn't
do.
I've grown up!
I've become my own person!
And you,
Oh you,
You are nothing to me,
Not even a blip on the radar of my world,
A shadow at the edge of my galaxy,
No more noticed,
Than a single snowflake in a storm,
I'm done with even the memory of you,
I am me and there is nothing,
And no one that can change that

Forgiveness

Forgiveness is not demanded,
Only freely given.

Hate

Hate is the most dangerous,
consuming our all

Joy

Joy is where we find the route,
To our happiness.

Sadness

It's ok to sad,
We all are at times,
Some days it's a good thing,
Working through the thoughts,
Hidden in your own mind,
Don't try to explain it,
Feelings are felt for a reason,
Just because you don't understand,
Doesn't mean they should be ignored

A Piece Lost

I miss you,
I don't even know why,
I don't even like you anymore,
I guess I miss your presence in my life,
You were such a large part of it,
For far too long.
After I left you,
I tried the wrong ways,
To fill that hole I ripped in myself,
But it was all the worst way that,
Made everything worse.
The only way I see,
Is to find a way to love myself for once.

Wings

Are we born with wings?
Wings that can carry us,
To our hidden dreams.
But many of us fall,
Locking our souls,
Inside a cage,
Of fear and pain.
A single crack,
Lets in a world,
Of light and air.
Breaking that cage,
Can let us soar once again.

Memories

The only power you hold,
Is the pain of my memories.

Mistake

I will never forget,
Why you were my mistake.

Goals

I will never be a memory,
If I don't make my mark.

Pushing Forward

Pain in my chest,
From the overwhelming emotion,
I know I was wrong,
But you wish you would talk to me,
I can only grow,
From knowing the truth.

Love or Lust

People treat love and lust,
Like completely different things,
Rather than two sides of the same coin.
One is emotional,
While the other is physical,
You can have one with the other,
But that doesn't preclude,
A combination of the pair.

Fake

I'd rather be lonely,
Than fake!

Progress

The concept of progress,
Is an interesting thing,
It's entirely subject to one's own beliefs.
Ones steady march forward,
Is another desperate leap backwards.
At times a fundamental shift in perception,
Can give the appearance of a lifetime of waste,
But was actually the step,
For another to take their charge.

Isolation

Self-isolation isn't so hard,
When you've spent your adult life,
Running in fear of being hurt…
Getting close to others is scary,
Will they be the next to turn their back?
Will they be the next to crush my heart?
Or will I push them away once again?

A Path Forwards

I'm lost,
No idea where...
No idea how…
I want to find a path,
A path I can make my own,
One to step into the future.
Find my lost passion,
Find my forgotten future,
I don't want to be lost anymore.

Stories

I wonder if stories are told,
About the crazy times of my life?
Are they forgotten with me,
Or are they tales told by others?
We all want to leave a legacy,
Be it good or bad.
Inside we all remember,
That once no one speaks about us,
We are truly forgotten.

Not Good Enough

I'm always afraid,
Of staying the same,
I don't want to be,
The me of the past,
I want to be,
Greater,
Smarter,
Wiser,
Nicer,
Just,
Better.

A Broken Stair

I was on the wrong path,
Not knowing what to do,
Lost in a place,
I didn't want to be,
I now face a choice,
To keep going,
Or fix what I broke,
Me.

Longing

Longing for a simpler time,
When we played in the streets,
And went home at dusk,
The only problems we saw,
Were the drama on tv,
Being shielded by our parents,
Keeping the innocence of a child.

Sin Eater

We try to protect those we love,
Be their sin eater if we must,
But there comes a time,
We must lift the wing,
Covering their eyes,
Letting them fly away,
Seeing the world,
With its shades of grey,
Strength is grown through adversity,
Only they can soar.

The Smith

The hammer blows,
Upon your soul,
Tearing free the weakness.

The dull iron left aside,
As the shining steel,
At your core,
Is released into the open.

ABOUT THE AUTHOR

C. R. Dunn is an Australian writer, author and part-time poet that spends more of his time reading other writers work than writing his own.

Thankyou for reading

www.ingramcontent.com/pod-product-compliance
Lightning Source LLC
La Vergne TN
LVHW041058150826
845673LV00007B/1833

* 9 7 9 8 3 5 3 2 7 4 7 7 3 *